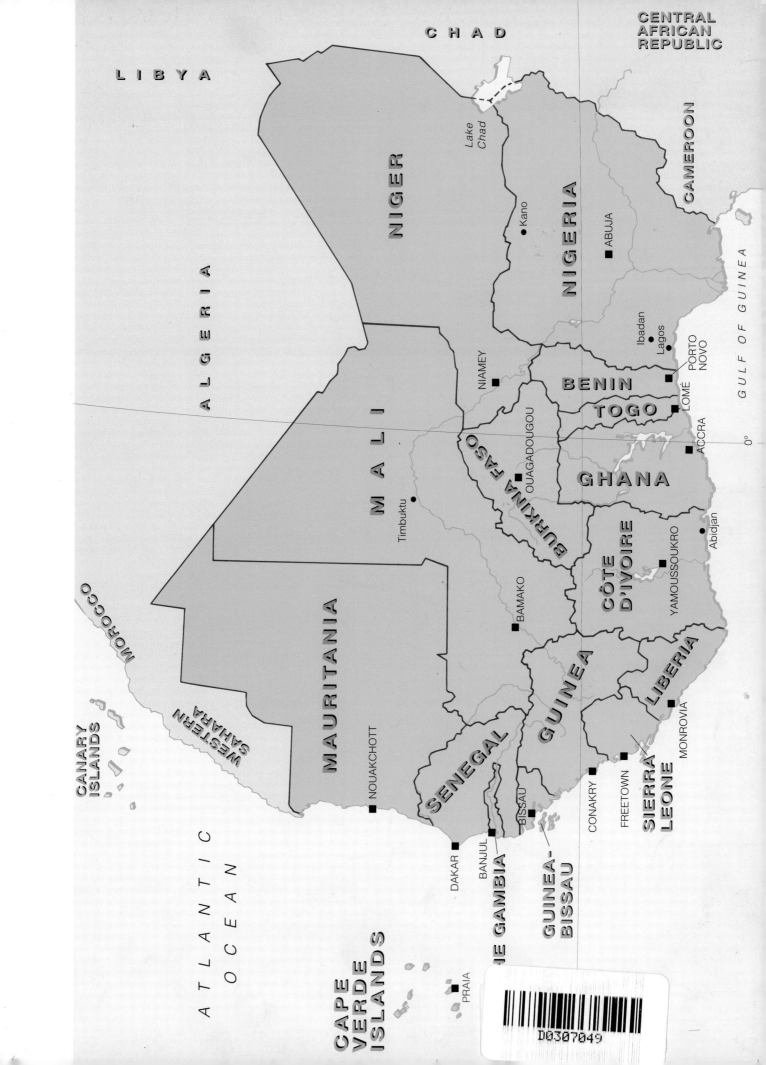

CENTRAL
AFRICAN
REPUBLIC

CHAD

LIBYA

NIGER

Lake
Chad

Kano

NIGERIA

■ ABUJA

CAMEROON

GULF OF GUINEA

ALGERIA

Ibadan
• *Lagos*

NIAMEY
■

PORTO
NOVO

BENIN

LOMÉ ■

TOGO

0°

MALI

BURKINA FASO

OUAGADOUGOU ■

GHANA

ACCRA ■

Timbuktu
•

CÔTE
D'IVOIRE

YAMOUSSOUKRO ■

Abidjan
•

MOROCCO

BAMAKO ■

GUINEA

LIBERIA

MAURITANIA

CANARY
ISLANDS

WESTERN
SAHARA

NOUAKCHOTT ■

SENEGAL

BISSAU ■

CONAKRY ■

FREETOWN ■

SIERRA
LEONE

MONROVIA ■

DAKAR ■

BANJUL ■

THE GAMBIA

GUINEA-
BISSAU

ATLANTIC
OCEAN

CAPE
VERDE
ISLANDS

PRAIA ■

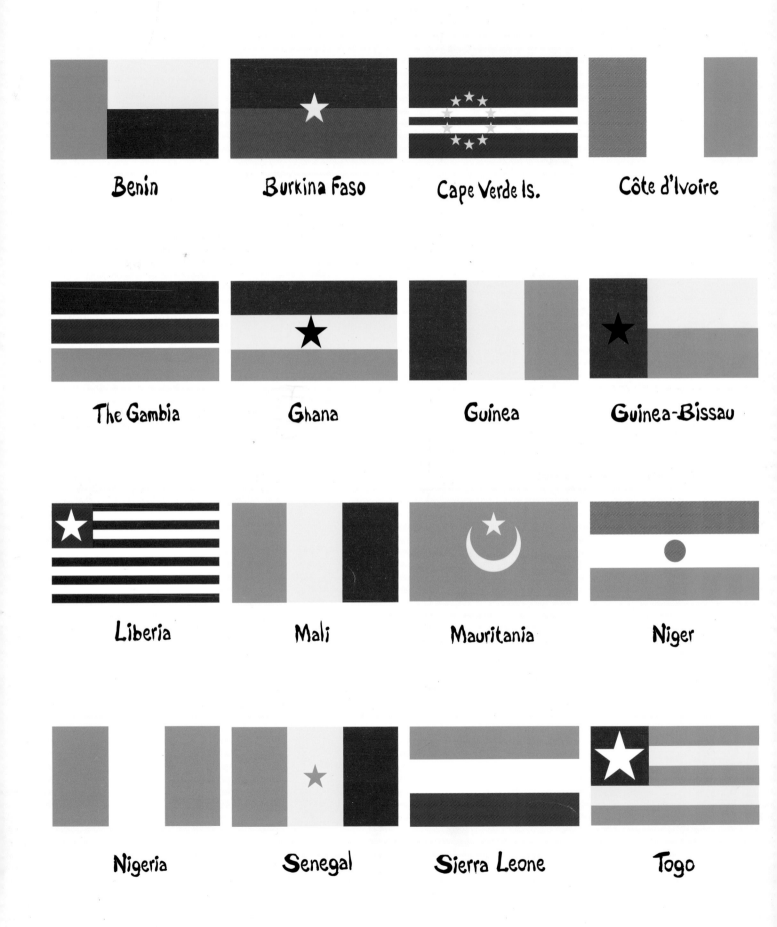

Benin

Burkina Faso

Cape Verde Is.

Côte d'Ivoire

The Gambia

Ghana

Guinea

Guinea-Bissau

Liberia

Mali

Mauritania

Niger

Nigeria

Senegal

Sierra Leone

Togo

WORLD FACT FILES

West Africa

Tony Binns and Rob Bowden

MACDONALD YOUNG BOOKS

First published in 1998 by Macdonald Young Books
An imprint of Wayland Publishers Ltd
© Macdonald Young Books 1998

Macdonald Young Books
61 Western Road
Hove
East Sussex
BN3 1JD

Find Macdonald Young Books on the Internet at
http://www.wayland.co.uk

Design and typesetting Roger Kohn Designs
Commissioning Editor Hazel Songhurst
Editor Merle Thompson
Picture research Shelley Noronha
Maps János Márffy

We are grateful to the following for permission
to reproduce photographs:
Front Cover: Panos *above*;
Axiom (James Morris) *below*
Axiom, pages 12 *below*, (James Morris), 18 (James Morris), 35
(James Morris), 37 (James Morris), 45 (James Morris); Tony
Binns, pages 34 *above*, 40, 42 left; Colorific, page 36 (Carl
Purcell); Eye Ubiquitous, pages 11 *above* (Thelma Sanders),
16 (Mark Newham), 17 (A Hibbert); FLPA, page 41 (E & D
Hosking); Getty Images, page 8 *below* (Steven Rothfield);
Robert Harding, page 12 *above*, 13, 19 *below*, 43; Impact,
pages 9 (Caroline Penn), 10 *above* (Carolyn Bates),
19 *above* (David Palmer), 22 (Caroline Penn), 23 *above*
(Caroline Penn), 32 (Caroline Penn), 33 (Caroline Penn),
42 *right* (David Palmer); Link, page 24 *above and below*
(Ron Giling); Panos, pages 14 (J Hartley), 20 (Bruce Paton),
25 (Betty Press), 27 (Liba Taylor), 28 *right* (Betty Press),
29 (Jon Spaull), 30 (Jeremy Hartley), 31 (Ron Giling),
34 *below* (Ron Giling), 38 *above* (Liba Taylor), 38 *below*
(Jeremy Hartley), 39 (Ian Cartwright), 44 (Betty Press);
John Spaull, pages, 10/11 *below*; Still Pictures, page 15
(Martin Wright); Topham, pages 26, 28 *left*; Werner Foreman,
page 8 *above*; WPL, page 21, 23 *below*.

The statistics given in this book are the most up to date
available at the time of going to press

Printed in Hong Kong by Wing King Tong

A CIP catalogue record for this book is available from
the British Library

ISBN: 0 7500 2433 X

**C
O
N
T
E
N
T
S**

Words that are explained in the glossary are printed in
SMALL CAPITALS the first time they are mentioned in the text.

⬛ INTRODUCTION

For the purpose of this book, West Africa is defined as the 16 countries that belong to the Economic Community of the West African States (ECOWAS). These are Benin, Burkina Faso, Cape Verde, Côte d'Ivoire, Ghana, Guinea, Guinea-Bissau, Liberia, Mali, Mauritania, Niger Republic, Nigeria, Senegal, Sierra Leone, The Gambia and Togo. All are countries on the African mainland, with the exception of Cape Verde, a group of islands in the Atlantic Ocean off the west coast of Mauritania and Senegal.

West Africa contains dense forests, vast expanses of desert and grassland, important wetland areas and many large sprawling cities. The region has a long

◀ *A sixteenth-century brass head of Idia, the Queen Mother of the Benin Kingdom in southern Nigeria. The Benin Kingdom has a great reputation for metalworking and there are many fine examples such as this.*

▼ *A Dogon village clinging to the lower slopes of the Bandiagara Escarpment in Mali. These densely settled villages stand between the plateau above, where intensive vegetable cultivation is practised, and the millet and sorghum fields on the plains below.*

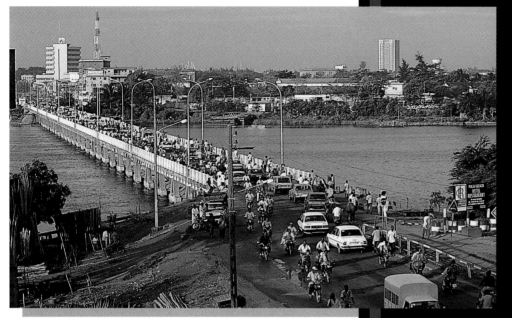

▲ *Rush hour in Cotonou, Benin. West Africa has many large cities that are growing much faster than the general population growth rates.*

- Total area: 6,131,390 square kilometres
- Total population (1995): 210.7 million
- Population density (1995): Average of 34 people per square kilometre (121 per square kilometre in Nigeria; 2 per square kilometre in Mauritania)
- Largest cities: Lagos 4,100,000; Abidjan 2,200,000; Dakar 1,730,000; Ibadan 2,000,000; Conakry 810,000; Bamako 746,000
- Longest river: Niger, 4,180 kilometres
- Largest lake: Lake Chad, 26,000 square kilometres
- Major resources: Oil, timber, bauxite, uranium, rutile (titanium dioxide)
- Major products: Cocoa, coffee, cotton
- Environmental problems: Soil erosion, DESERTIFICATION, water shortages

and rich cultural history. During the Middle Ages, West Africa already had long-established trade routes across the great Sahara Desert. Trading centres along the desert's southern edge, such as Kano, Timbuktu, Djenne and Mopti thrived. Metal bars and cowrie shells were used as currency. A number of powerful states controlled parts of the SAVANNA and sahel and, further south in the forest, sophisticated mining and metal-working kingdoms existed in Ashanti and Benin.

From the 16th to the 19th centuries, West Africa supplied millions of slaves. They were gathered together in forts along the coast, before being transferred by ship to the Caribbean and the southern states of the USA to work on plantations. Many died in the appalling conditions on the journey. From the mid-19th century, West Africa was gradually divided among the European powers. A period of about 80 years of

COLONIALISM followed, during which education, health and legal systems were introduced. Vast quantities of mineral resources and CASH CROPS were sent to Europe during this period.

Today, more than 30 years after most countries gained INDEPENDENCE, West Africa is probably the poorest region in the world. Living standards are often extremely low, and unstable political and economic conditions have prevented any improvement in the lives of most people. But it is a fascinating region, with great potential, and this book explores its people, environments and future prospects.

THE LANDSCAPE

One of the most striking things about the West African region is its varied landscape. Moving northwards from the Nigerian coast, the landscape changes from the mangroves of the Niger Delta, into the tropical forests of southern Nigeria, the savanna bushland around Abuja and, finally, into savanna grassland around the northern city of Kano. Crossing into the Niger Republic, the conditions become increasingly ARID and we move into a landscape known as the sahel. This is an Arabic word meaning the 'shore', in this case the shore of the great Sahara Desert. These distinct environmental zones, roughly parallel to the coast, are characteristic of most of West Africa.

The 16 West African countries vary greatly in size, ranging from the tiny Cape

◀ *The Bandiagara escarpment in Dogon country, south-east Mali, is over 150 kilometres long and is a major upland feature in this part of West Africa.*

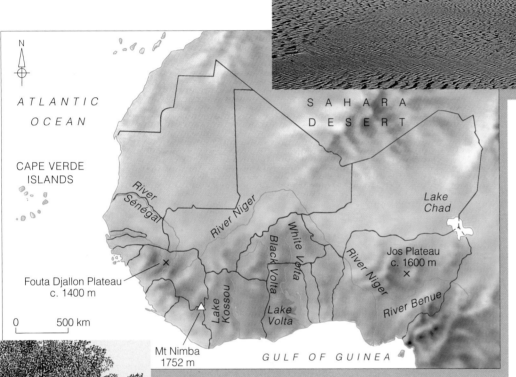

▲ *The Sahara Desert covers large parts of the northern areas of West Africa. This is a typical scene of sand dunes and a desert oasis in Mauritania. Some areas of the desert are much stonier than this.*

◀ *Mangrove swamps in Sierra Leone. The dense mangrove vegetation thrives in the salty water of the creeks and estuaries of rivers. Mangroves grow on stilt roots to keep their leaves above the high tide level.*

Verde Islands (4,030 square kilometres) to the vast desert state of Niger Republic (1,267,000 square kilometres). Burkina Faso, Mali and Niger are the only LAND-LOCKED states in West Africa. The rest share the Atlantic coastline. The shapes of several of the states are unusual because their boundaries were drawn up by European colonial powers in the Treaty of Berlin in 1885. Mali, for example, has straight borders with Mauritania and Algeria while Togo and Benin are long and narrow.

Most of West Africa consists of low-lying plains and basins that rarely exceed 500 metres above sea level. However, there are a few significant upland areas such as the

◀ *The River Niger is an important source of fish and water for irrigation. It also acts as a transport route in inland areas such as the Niger Republic.*

Fouta Djallon Plateau in Guinea, the Jos and Mambila Plateaux in Nigeria and the Freetown Peninsula in Sierra Leone. These plateaux range between 800–1500 metres, but rising above these are mountain peaks such as Bintumani (1,948 metres) in Sierra Leone and Dimlang (2,040 metres) on the Nigeria–Cameroon border.

West Africa's major river is the River Niger which, with a length of 4,180 kilometres, is the third longest river in Africa. It rises in the Fouta Djallon Plateau of Guinea in the west of the region, flows northwards through Mali to Timbuktu, then bends sharply south through Niger Republic and into Nigeria. There it is joined from the east by the Benue River (1,370 kilometres) about 500 kilometres from the coast. The Niger is unusual in having two DELTAS, the so called 'inland delta' of Mali and the coastal delta in Nigeria. The inland delta is one of the major wetlands of Africa. Irrigated rice and cotton are grown and fish are caught locally. Other major rivers in the region are the Senegal (1,610 kilometres), the Volta (1,448 kilometres) and the Gambia (1,125 kilometres).

The two largest lakes in West Africa are Lake Chad bordering Nigeria and Niger

▲ *Rainforest once covered much of the southern parts of West Africa but, today, most has been destroyed for farming or timber extraction. Here, rainforest in Cross River State, Nigeria, can be seen regenerating after a period of cultivation.*

KEY FACTS

● The largest mainland country in West Africa, Niger, is 112 times bigger than The Gambia which is the smallest.

● With an area of 103,000 square kilometres, the inland Niger Delta in Mali is almost as big as the combined areas of Belgium, The Netherlands and Switzerland.

● Lake Volta stretches over 400 kilometres from the Akosombo Dam into the northern savanna interior of Ghana, providing fishing and water for irrigating crops.

● The Niger Delta in Nigeria is the largest in Africa, covering an area of about 36,300 square kilometres and with a coastline of almost 190 kilometres.

● In the 15th century, Portuguese sailors thought that the mountains of the Freetown peninsula resembled a sleeping lion. They called them 'Serra Lyoa', meaning 'lion mountains'. The name later chosen for the country was Sierra Leone.

Republic, and Lake Volta in Ghana. Lake Chad is a natural lake covering an area of 26,000 square kilometres. Lake Volta (8,500 square kilometres) was created in 1966 when the Akosombo Dam was built across the River Volta to generate HYDRO-ELECTRICITY.

The West African coastline stretches for 5,100 kilometres and shelves gently into the sea. There are many sand bars and LAGOONS and few harbours suitable for large ships. Freetown is a rare example of a natural deep-water harbour. The other major ports in West Africa, such as Lagos and Abidjan, have only developed after large-scale construction work. Lagos is reached through a lagoon that requires regular dredging and the Vridi Canal had to be cut through a sand bar to allow access to Abidjan.

▼ *A beach outside Lomé, in Togo. West Africa's coastline has many wide sandy beaches with great potential for the development of tourism. Many beaches are fringed with coconut palms. The shells of the coconuts are often used as fuel in neighbouring towns and cities.*

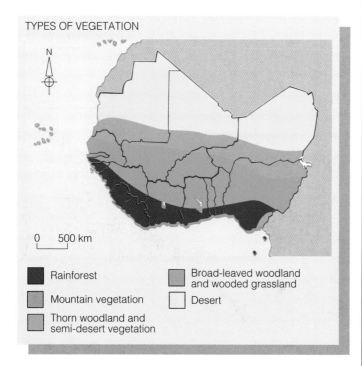

The Harmattan is a major feature of the West African climate. Localized dust storms, such as this one in Burkina Faso, are common prior to the arrival of the rains.

Rainfall is the key factor in shaping West Africa's different environmental zones. As a general rule, inland from the coast the climate becomes drier, but some upland areas have higher rainfall and lower temperatures than the surrounding lowlands. On the coast, the region has a single distinct rainy season between May and October, but at the edge of the Sahara Desert, the rainy season is shorter (June/July to August/September) and much less reliable. Timbuktu, for example, receives just over 200 mm of rain annually.

TYPES OF VEGETATION

N

0   500 km

- ■ Rainforest
- ■ Mountain vegetation
- ■ Thorn woodland and semi-desert vegetation
- ■ Broad-leaved woodland and wooded grassland
- □ Desert

KEY FACTS

● Freetown's annual rainfall (3,434 mm) is almost four times that of Manchester, UK (859 mm) and more than three times that of New York (1,092 mm).

● Parts of Nigeria and Sierra Leone can experience over 210 thunderstorms per year and the largest storms may last over eight hours.

● In colonial times, West Africa was known as 'The White Man's Grave' due to the disease, heat and humidity. The cool Harmattan wind, which was sometimes called 'The African Doctor', provided the only relief.

● The savanna and the sahel regions had major droughts in the 1910s, 1940s and 1970s. The rains were below average every year between 1970 and 1990.

Almost all of this falls in the four months from June to September.

Parts of the West African coast, by contrast, receive more rainfall than almost anywhere else in Africa. Freetown, the capital of Sierra Leone, has an annual rainfall of 3,434 mm compared with 958 mm in Nairobi, (Kenya), and 508 mm in Cape Town (South Africa). Most of Freetown's

rain falls between April and November and, with temperatures approaching 30°C, humidity is extremely high. The beginning and end of the rainy season are characterized by spectacular storms, often with strong winds, thunder and lightning.

Temperatures across West Africa are high throughout the year and the average monthly temperature never falls below 18°C. In general, the temperature range is least near the coast and increases inland. The greatest ranges in temperature occur during the Harmattan period, when daytime temperatures may be over 40°C, sometimes falling to below 6°C at night in inland areas. The Harmattan is a dry dusty wind, bringing cool air south from the Sahara Desert between December and March. It can even reach the coast for short periods. The dust can be so thick that cars need to use their headlights in the middle of the day and people suffer from cracked skin and colds.

◀ *Thunder storms with torrential rain are typical at the beginning of the rainy season. They can cause flash floods that disrupt transport and make some roads impassable.*

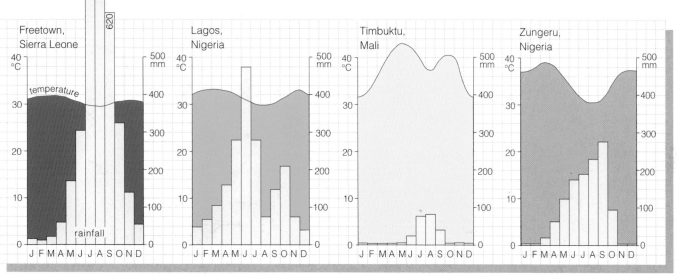

NATURAL RESOURCES

West Africa is rich in mineral resources such as oil, coal and tin in Nigeria, bauxite in Guinea, gold in Ghana, diamonds and rutile in Sierra Leone, iron ore in Mauritania, and uranium in Niger. Many of these resources are in remote areas, making them difficult or expensive to extract, and any POLITICAL INSTABILITY in the region can interrupt production. Some minerals are produced in significant amounts, for example Guinea is the world's second biggest producer of bauxite, which is used in the production of aluminium, and Niger is the second largest producer of uranium after Canada.

Nigeria is Africa's largest producer of oil, which was first extracted from wells in the Niger Delta in the late 1950s. Production increased significantly in the early 1970s and, since 1973, oil has accounted for over 90% of Nigeria's total export earnings.

Some 70–80% of West Africans still rely on wood for fuel, and in rural areas wood is often the only available source of energy. In urban areas, electricity, generated from hydro-electric power stations such as Akosombo Dam in Ghana, supplies the needs of industry and wealthier households. But, even in large cities, many poorer people rely on wood brought in from surrounding rural areas. Timber is also exported and West Africa accounts for 6.4% of world production, with Nigeria alone accounting for 3.5% in 1993. In the 1970s, natural rubber was produced in Liberia, and a vast plantation was owned by the

▼ *The Akosombo Dam in Ghana, which is situated at the southern end of Lake Volta. Hydro-electric power is an important source of electricity in some West African countries.*

▶ *Bark is stripped from hardwood tree trunks at Abidjan harbour, Côte d'Ivoire. Timber production is important to local economies but, uncontrolled, it can lead to severe environmental damage.*

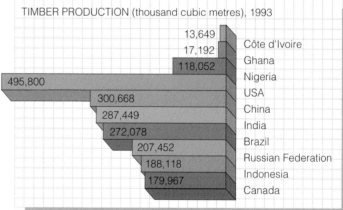

KEY FACTS

● In 1970, Sierra Leone produced 2,050,000 thousand carats of diamonds. In 1993, production had fallen to 350,000 carats.

● In 1994, Ghana, formerly Gold Coast, was the world's ninth biggest producer of gold. In pre-colonial times, the Ashanti region in south-western Ghana, with its capital Kumasi, was referred to as 'the Kingdom of Gold'.

● In 1970, Guinea produced 2,642 thousand tonnes of bauxite; in 1994 this figure had increased by more than 500% to 13,761 thousand tonnes.

TIMBER PRODUCTION (thousand cubic metres), 1993

13,649	Côte d'Ivoire
17,192	Ghana
118,052	Nigeria
495,800	USA
300,668	China
287,449	India
272,078	Brazil
207,452	Russian Federation
188,118	Indonesia
179,967	Canada

OIL PRODUCTION, (thousand tonnes), 1994

91,045 Nigeria
119,030 UK
139,615 Mexico
146,082 China
179,444 Iran
315,764 Russian Federation
335,972 USA
401,197 Saudi Arabia

BAUXITE PRODUCTION, (thousand tonnes), 1994

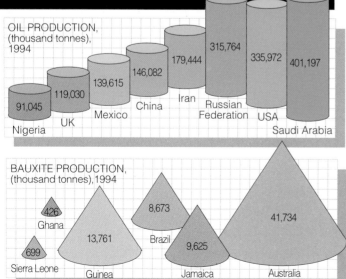

426 Ghana
699 Sierra Leone
13,761 Guinea
8,673 Brazil
9,625 Jamaica
41,734 Australia

Firestone Company. More recently, Liberia's civil war and continuing political unrest have interrupted production.

The land remains the basic resource for most people and is used to grow food crops such as rice, maize, millet, yams and cassava, and also important cash crops such as cocoa, coffee, cotton, and groundnuts. The importance of land as a resource is reflected by the fact that so many of the region's major exports are agricultural commodities.

POPULATION

In 1995, the total population of West Africa was just over 210 million. But population is unevenly distributed with 53% of people living in just one country, Nigeria, which covers only 15% of the region's total land area. With 111.7 million people, Nigeria has more people than any other African country. Its closest rivals are Egypt with 62.9 million

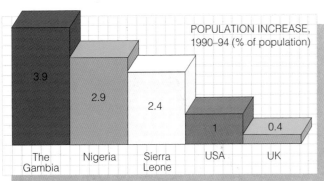

POPULATION INCREASE, 1990–94 (% of population)

The Gambia	Nigeria	Sierra Leone	USA	UK
3.9	2.9	2.4	1	0.4

▲ *West Africa has a wealth of traditional cultures. These musicians in Nigeria are helping to preserve such traditions from one generation to another.*

and Ethiopia with 55.1 million. In sharp contrast, Cape Verde has only 372,000 people and both The Gambia and Guinea-Bissau each have 1.1 million. Even massive countries like Niger and Mauritania have only relatively small populations, with 9.2 million and 2.3 million respectively. Nigeria has 121 people per square kilometre, whereas Niger has 7 and Mauritania only 2. For further comparison, the UK has a population density of 241 people per square kilometre and the USA has 28.

◀ *The ancient city of Kano in northern Nigeria, is densely settled. It includes a number of pits from which building materials have been excavated. They are now filled with water and have become a serious health hazard since they are a breeding ground for mosquitoes.*

Population growth rates in West Africa are among the highest in the world, only exceeded by Middle Eastern states such as Jordan and Yemen. The Gambia had an average annual growth rate of 3.9% between 1990 and 1994 and Côte d'Ivoire recorded 3.6% over the same period. Even Guinea Bissau, with the lowest growth rate of 2%, has a rate that is double the USA growth rate and five times that of the UK.

URBANIZATION

Although the West African region is still predominantly rural, towns and cities are growing more rapidly than the general population. Burkina Faso, for example, almost doubled its average urban growth rate each year from 5.5% between 1965

▶ *Lagos is West Africa's largest city with around 4,100,000 inhabitants. Modern high-rise tower blocks dominate the colonial buildings in the foreground. The harbour can be seen in the distance.*

It is common for people throughout West Africa to live in large extended family groups. This family compound in Ghana is home to a man with several wives and many children.

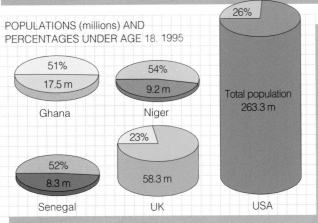

POPULATIONS (millions) AND PERCENTAGES UNDER AGE 18. 1995

Ghana 51% 17.5 m

Niger 54% 9.2 m

Senegal 52% 8.3 m

UK 23% 58.3 m

USA 26% Total population 263.3 m

history. Timbuktu, for example, was founded around 1000 AD and became an important religious and educational centre, with the first university in West Africa. Further east, in what is now northern Nigeria, Kano had 75,000 inhabitants in the

and 1980, to 10.4% between 1980 and 1995. One of the causes of this very rapid growth of towns is the movement of people from rural areas, a process called RURAL—URBAN MIGRATION The towns and cities cannot grow fast enough to cope with this migration and people have started building their own homes out of basic materials on the outskirts of many large settlements. These 'shanty towns' are often very crowded, without fresh water or proper sanitation.

Unlike other parts of Africa, many towns and cities in West Africa have a long

KEY FACTS

● Mauritania and the Cape Verde Islands are the most urbanized countries in the region. In 1992, around 50% of the population were living in towns and cities.
● In Nigeria alone, no fewer than 395 different languages have been identified. In some cases a single language, such as Yoruba, may have many dialects.
● Elmina Castle was built on the Ghanaian coast by the Portuguese in the late-15th century. It is the oldest and largest of more than 20 fortifications built by the European powers to house slaves awaiting ships to take them across the Atlantic.

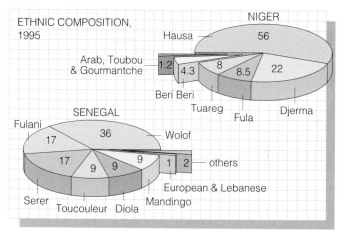

Men dressed in their best clothes sit and chat after attending Friday prayers at a mosque in northern Nigeria.

16th century. In south-western Nigeria, Ile-Ife, the spiritual capital of the Yoruba people was established by the 10th century and, later, many other large towns developed. Today Yorubaland is probably the most urbanized part of the African continent.

ETHNIC GROUPS AND LANGUAGES

West Africa is among the most diverse ethnic regions in the world. Possibly more languages are spoken here than in any other region of similar size. Although, in the colonial period, French, English and Portuguese were 'official' languages, tribal languages have remained very strong. This is because, unlike other parts of Africa, there were few European settlers in the region. Arabic is widely spoken throughout West Africa, particularly in the savanna and sahel regions. Although there are several hundred distinct ethnic groups in the region, they can be divided into three main cultural groups. The largest group consists of CULTIVATORS, such as the Mandinka in Senegal and The Gambia,

ETHNIC COMPOSITION, 1995

NIGER
Hausa 56
Arab, Toubou & Gourmantche 1.2
4.3
8
8.5
22
Beri Beri
Tuareg
Fula
Djerma

SENEGAL
Fulani 17
36
Wolof
17
9
9
9
1
2
others
Serer
Toucouleur
Diola
Mandingo
European & Lebanese

the Yoruba in Nigeria, the Mende in Sierra Leone and the Ashante in Ghana. The two smaller groups are the PASTORALISTS, such as the Fulani in the savanna region and the Tuareg further north towards the Sahara Desert, and fishing communities, such as the Ewe of Ghana and Togo and the Fanti of Ghana. Other, urban-based, groups are associated with crafts and light industries, and include the Yoruba and the famous metal workers of the ancient Benin Kingdom, located around Benin City in southern Nigeria.

DAILY LIFE

POVERTY

There are some elements of daily life that are common throughout West Africa. Poverty is the overwhelming issue. Four out of the five poorest countries in the world are located in the region, Niger being the poorest. The poverty of the region is highlighted by the fact that Sierra Leone has the world's lowest life expectancy of just 40 years and Niger the world's highest infant mortality rate of nearly 20%. Burkina Faso and Niger have the highest rates of adult illiteracy at over 80%, and the lowest ratio of doctors to population in the world. There is only one doctor for every 57,000 people in Burkina Faso. This is equivalent to a city the size of London having about 120 doctors.

URBAN LIFE

Not all West Africa's people are poor, however, and in every city there are wealthy business people and others with a high standard of living. The gap between rich and poor is large and often clearly visible. In Guinea Bissau for example, the wealthiest 20% of the population have

▲ *Workers' houses near a manganese mine in Ghana. Townships often grow up close to areas where cash crops are grown or adjacent to mines.*

nearly 60% of the country's wealth, whereas the poorest 40% have less than 10%. This means that, even in the cities, the great majority of people are very poor, living in overcrowded housing with inadequate facilities and a high risk of disease, illness and crime. Most of these people are, however, very enterprising and positive. Many of them work in the INFORMAL SECTOR of the economy selling papers, shining shoes, washing windscreens, working in back-street industries or selling produce brought in from the surrounding rural areas.

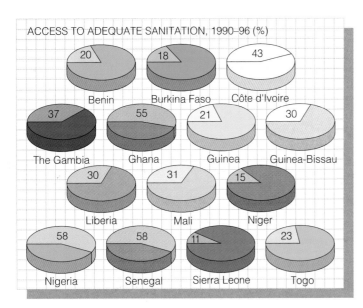

ACCESS TO ADEQUATE SANITATION, 1990–96 (%)

20	18	43
Benin	Burkina Faso	Côte d'Ivoire
37	55	21	30
The Gambia	Ghana	Guinea	Guinea-Bissau
30	31	15	
Liberia	Mali	Niger	
58	58	11	23
Nigeria	Senegal	Sierra Leone	Togo

◀ *Adults and children alike are taught basic healthcare at a rural workshop in Sierra Leone. People's health is generally very poor in West Africa, particularly in rural areas.*

RURAL LIFE

For most people who live in rural areas, daily life revolves around working on the land to earn their living. This may involve large-scale commercial farming, but is more likely to mean working on the small family farm, or herding livestock between water holes and pasture and selling milk in exchange for vegetables in rural markets.

The extended family live together in one household, which is responsible for

INFANT MORTALITY, 1995 (deaths under 1 year old per 1000)	
4	Japan
6	UK
8	USA
86	Burkina Faso
128	Guinea
134	Guinea Bissau
144	Liberia
164	Sierra Leone
191	Niger

providing food and income for all its members. Households commonly include mother, father, grandparents, unmarried relatives and many children for, under Moslem tradition, men may have up to four wives.

▶ *Football is an obsession throughout much of West Africa. Boys, like these in Nigeria, take advantage of any open space to practise their game.*

◄ In rural West Africa, the traditional walled family compound with a group of thatched huts is still a common feature of the landscape.

RELIGION AND EDUCATION

Islam is the most widespread religion in West Africa. In Senegal, for example, 92% of the population are Moslem and in Nigeria, the most heavily populated country, around 50% of the population are Moslem. Christianity, introduced by colonial missionaries in the 19th century, is also important, particularly in the south of the region in countries such as Ghana and

► Hundreds of people at Friday afternoon prayers in Ouagadougou, the capital of Burkina Faso. Mosques are a distinctive feature in most West African towns and cities.

RELIGIONS (%)

Moslem

Indigenous

Christian

NIGERIA — 50, 40, 10

MALI — 90, 9, 1

SIERRA LEONE — 60, 30, 10

SENEGAL — 92, 6, 2

GHANA — 30, 24, 38, 8 other

BENIN — 15, 15, 70

LIBERIA — 20, 10, 70

◀ *Children, in Mali, carrying their desks to school at the start of a new term. Even those lucky enough to go to school may still have to bring their own equipment.*

ADULT ILLITERACY, 1995 (%)

63 Benin	81 Burkina Faso	60 Côte d'Ivoire
61 The Gambia	36 Ghana	64 Guinea / 45 Guinea Bissau
66 Liberia	69 Mali	62 Mauritania
86 Niger	43 Nigeria	67 Senegal / 69 Sierra Leone
48 Togo	less than 5 UK	less than 5 USA

Nigeria. Many communities, particularly in rural areas, hold on to their traditional religions and beliefs. The highest proportion of these is found in Benin (around 70%).

Education is regarded as a privilege among West Africans, and although about 70% of children attend primary school, the numbers staying on beyond this level are very small. In strongly Moslem communities, there is a tendency for girls to stay at home with their mothers, so levels of female education and literacy are often well below those of males. In Mauritania, for example, where over 90% of people are Moslem, 50% of males are literate compared with only 26% of females.

KEY FACTS

● Giving and receiving kola nuts is a traditional exchange of friendship. These chestnut-sized nuts with a bitter taste are chewed and have the same effect as caffeine in tea and coffee.
● During 1994, in Guinea Bissau, 77% of boys and 42% of girls were enrolled in primary school. At secondary level, the figures fell to just 9% for boys and 4% for girls.
● In countries like Togo and Benin, items such as televisions are a luxury. In 1993, there were only 6 sets per 1000 people compared with 60 in Côte d'Ivoire, the highest in the region, or 813 in the USA – the highest level in the world.

FESTIVALS

West Africans celebrate a large number of festivals. Probably the most important are the Moslem festival of Eid-al-Fitr, celebrating the end of the month-long fast of Ramadan, and the Christian festivals of Christmas and Easter. Other festivals are associated with the farming calendar, such as the New Yam festival, celebrated by Nigeria's Yoruba people at harvest time.

RULE AND LAW

Before independence, the 16 countries of West Africa were colonial territories belonging to three European powers, Britain, France and Portugal. The only exception to this is Liberia, which has been an independent state since it was set up in 1847. Liberia's origins go back to the American Colonization Society, founded in 1816, to settle black Americans in Africa, from where many of their ancestors had been taken as slaves. Liberia has maintained close links with the USA. It was founded with an American-style constitution and the capital city Monrovia was named after US President Monroe. The black settlers became known as 'Americo–Liberians', and have quite different cultural characteristics from other African cultural groups in Liberia.

In the neighbouring country, Sierra Leone, the British similarly moved groups of freed black slaves, known as Creoles, from Caribbean plantations. The city of Freetown is located on the spot where they were settled. Like the Americo–Liberians, the Creoles have a distinct culture compared with other Sierra Leonean peoples.

It was West Africa that led the way to African independence south of the Sahara. The first country to be granted independence was Gold Coast, renamed Ghana in 1957, under the dynamic leadership of Kwame Nkrumah. Many West

▲ *In August 1983, Captain Thomas Sankara, a young army officer, seized power in Burkina Faso with his National Revolutionary Council. He was one of many young military leaders who emerged in West Africa after independence.*

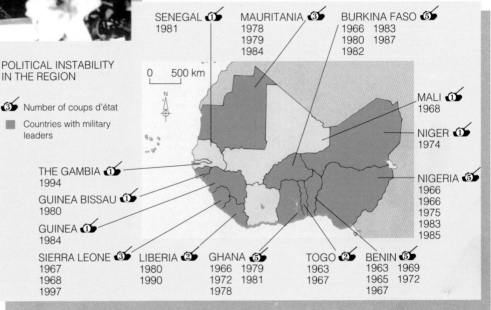

POLITICAL INSTABILITY IN THE REGION

3 Number of coups d'état

■ Countries with military leaders

0   500 km

SENEGAL **1**
1981

MAURITANIA **3**
1978
1979
1984

BURKINA FASO **5**
1966   1983
1980   1987
1982

MALI **1**
1968

NIGER **1**
1974

NIGERIA **5**
1966
1966
1975
1983
1985

THE GAMBIA **1**
1994

GUINEA BISSAU **1**
1980

GUINEA **1**
1984

SIERRA LEONE **3**
1967
1968
1997

LIBERIA **2**
1980
1990

GHANA **5**
1966   1979
1972   1981
1978

TOGO **2**
1963
1967

BENIN **5**
1963   1969
1965   1972
1967

◀ *In 1995, Liberia was beginning to emerge from a decade of turmoil and civil war. Many civilians lost their lives and children as young as 14 were recruited to fight as soldiers.*

African countries quickly followed Ghana in gaining independence. All the French colonial states were granted independence in 1960, and have retained strong links with France. The exception was Guinea, which gained independence in 1958 and cut many of its connections with France. Following Ghana, Britain's other West African

KEY FACTS

● Nigeria has the biggest military force in West Africa with 76,500 troops in 1994, compared with just 800 in The Gambia.
● The disruption caused by civil war in Liberia reduced the GROSS NATIONAL PRODUCT (GNP) PER CAPITA from US$ 699 in 1991 to just US$ 390 in 1995. Iron ore production fell from 12.9 million tonnes in 1988 to 1.7 million in 1992.
● Leopold Senghor became Senegal's first president at independence in 1960, but he stepped down from power voluntarily in 1980. Senghor is well known for his poetry and writing on 'negritude', in which he considers the significance of being black and celebrates African civilization and values.

INDEPENDENCE

REPUBLIC OF BENIN
formerly **Dahomey**
former colonial power: **France**
Independence: **1 August 1960**

BURKINA FASO
formerly **Upper Volta**
former colonial power: **France**
Independence: **5 August 1960**

REPUBLIC OF CAPE VERDE
formerly **Cape Verde Islands**
former colonial power: **Portugal**
Independence: **5 July 1975**

REPUBLIC OF CÔTE D'IVOIRE
formerly **Côte d'Ivoire**
former colonial power: **France**
Independence: **7 August 1960**

REPUBLIC OF THE GAMBIA
formerly **Gambia**
former colonial power: **Britain**
Independence: **18 February 1965**

REPUBLIC OF GHANA
formerly **Gold Coast**
former colonial power: **Britain**
Independence: **6 March 1957**

REPUBLIC OF GUINEA
formerly **French Guinea**
former colonial power: **France**
Independence: **12 October 1958**

REPUBLIC OF GUINEA-BISSAU
formerly **Portuguese Guinea**
former colonial power: **Portugal**
Independence: **10 September 1974**

REPUBLIC OF LIBERIA
formerly un-named
former colonial power: **None**
Independence: **26 July 1847**

REPUBLIC OF MALI
formerly **French Sudan**
former colonial power: **France**
Independence: **22 September 1960**

ISLAMIC REPUBLIC OF MAURITANIA
formerly **Mauritania**
former colonial power: **France**
Independence: **28 November 1960**

REPUBLIC OF NIGER
formerly **Niger**
former colonial power: **France**
Independence: **3 August 1960**

FEDERAL REPUBLIC OF NIGERIA
formerly **Nigeria**
former colonial power: **Britain**
Independence: **1 October 1960**

REPUBLIC OF SENEGAL
formerly **Senegal**
former colonial power: **France**
Independence: **20 August 1960**

REPUBLIC OF SIERRA LEONE
formerly **Sierra Leone**
former colonial power: **Britain**
Independence: **24 April 1961**

REPUBLIC OF TOGO
formerly **French Togo**
former colonial power: **France/Germany**
Independence: **27 April 1960**

territories of Nigeria, Sierra Leone, and The Gambia, were granted independence in 1960, 1961 and 1965 respectively. The last countries to receive their independence were the two small Portuguese territories of Guinea-Bissau and Cape Verde in 1974 and 1975.

At independence, a number of West African states seemed to have a bright future, but nearly all have suffered from some degree of unstable government. Often one government has been overthrown by another and military regimes have replaced civilian democracies or vice versa. Some countries have had five or more military coups since independence, notably Benin, Burkina Faso, Ghana and Nigeria. The West African states need to develop strong economies if they are to compete effectively on the world markets, but continuing political unrest can make this hard to achieve. The unstable political situation in Nigeria, for example, has prevented the country from developing what could be one of the strongest economies in Africa. Certain other states, like Ghana, have managed to overcome long periods of instability. Under the leadership of Jerry Rawlings, Ghana has made considerable economic progress during the 1980s and 1990s.

◀ *Ghana was the first state in West Africa to gain independence in March 1957. Its popular leader, Kwame Nkrumah, had great visions of a united independent Africa.*

▼ *Jerry Rawlings, who seized power in Ghana as a military leader, later won a democratic election as a civilian candidate in November 1992, taking 58% of the vote.*

ECOWAS
(The Economic Community of West African States)

ECOWAS was established at the Treaty of Lagos, which was signed in May 1975

BENIN
BURKINA FASO
CAPE VERDE
CÔTE D'IVOIRE
THE GAMBIA

TOGO
SIERRA LEONE
SENEGAL
NIGERIA
NIGER

THE CHAIRMAN
(elected annually from the member states in turn)

THE CONFERENCE OF HEADS OF STATE AND GOVERNMENT
The highest authority of ECOWAS (meets once a year)

THE TRIBUNAL
Interprets Treaty and settles disputes between member states

THE COUNCIL OF MINISTERS
Consists of 2 representatives from each country

THE EXECUTIVE SECRETARIAT
The Executive Secretary is elected for a 4-year term

6 specialized commissions
1 Trade, Customs, Immigration, Monetary & Payments
2 Industry, Agriculture, & Natural Resources
3 Transport, Communications & Energy
4 Social & Cultural Affairs
5 Administration & Finance
6 Information

FUND FOR CO-OPERATION, COMPENSATION, & DEVELOPMENT

GHANA | GUINEA | GUINEA BISSAU | LIBERIA | MALI | MAURITANIA

16 Member States

played a key role in resolving several of the region's conflicts, such as that in Liberia. ECOWAS has great potential, but there is some concern in the region that the organization is too heavily dominated by Nigeria.

ECOWAS

Nkrumah and other political figures felt that, with so many states in the region, some of them quite small, there was an urgent need for them to co-operate with one another along the lines of the European Economic Community (EEC). Three years after Nkrumah's death, the Treaty of Lagos was signed in May 1975 by 15 West African states. This set up the Economic Community of West African States (ECOWAS). Cape Verde became the sixteenth member two years later in 1977. ECOWAS aims to promote 'the rapid and balanced development of West Africa' and remove barriers to trade and commerce in order to create greater unity. The ECOWAS states have established an international military force called ECOMOG (the ECOWAS Monitoring Group). This has

▶ *Political supporters of the opposition party celebrate the opening of the new parliament in Freetown, Sierra Leone, after democratic elections were held in 1996.*

FOOD AND FARMING

CASH CROPS

Farming is the main activity in West Africa, employing over 70% of the population. The region is an important producer of cocoa, coffee, groundnuts (peanuts) and cotton. West Africa produces over half the world's cocoa beans, and Côte d'Ivoire is the world's largest producing country. Côte d'Ivoire is also the world's ninth largest producer of coffee, and Nigeria and Senegal are the fourth and sixth largest producers of groundnuts. Other important exported commodities include cotton from Mali, Côte d'Ivoire and Nigeria.

These crops are known as cash crops, which means they are mainly grown for sale on the world markets rather than for consumption by local people. Cash crops are normally worth more money than local crops, but there is always a risk that prices will fall due to changing world demands.

▲ *Intensive vegetable cultivation is becoming increasingly common in West Africa, particularly beside large rivers such as the Niger. The vegetables are sold in urban markets or exported.*

KEY FACTS

● Much of Cape Verde is dry and barren so large quantities of food are imported. The country's fishing industry, however, employs over 3,000 people and provides valuable export earnings.

● Nigeria, Côte d'Ivoire, Benin, Ghana and Togo are the world's top five producers of Yams. In 1993, they produced 25,242,000 tonnes or 89.7% of world production.

● In the pastoral countries of West Africa, livestock are more important than crops. In 1993, Mali had over 5.5 million cattle and Mauritania had nearly 1 million camels.

● In 1992, none of the West African states used more than 8 kilograms of fertilizer per hectare of agricultural land. This compares with 44 kilograms in the USA.

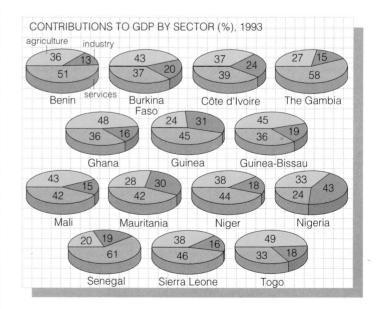

CONTRIBUTIONS TO GDP BY SECTOR (%), 1993

agriculture · industry · services

Country	agriculture	industry	services
Benin	36	13	51
Burkina Faso	43	20	37
Côte d'Ivoire	37	24	39
The Gambia	27	15	58
Ghana	48	16	36
Guinea	24	31	45
Guinea-Bissau	45	19	36
Mali	43	15	42
Mauritania	28	30	42
Niger	38	18	44
Nigeria	33	43	24
Senegal	20	19	61
Sierra Leone	38	16	46
Togo	49	18	33

▼ *Women, head-loading beans, walk past an irrigation gantry watering a field of sugar cane. Because of the seasonal shortages of water, large-scale irrigation is vital to commercial agriculture in West Africa.*

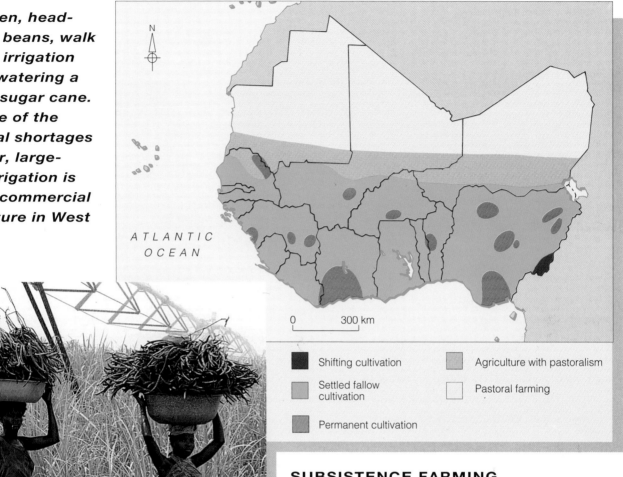

ATLANTIC OCEAN

N

0   300 km

■ Shifting cultivation

■ Settled fallow cultivation

■ Permanent cultivation

■ Agriculture with pastoralism

□ Pastoral farming

SUBSISTENCE FARMING

Although agricultural produce makes a valuable contribution to a country's economy, the main aim of most West African farmers is to feed their families. A wide range of food crops are grown. The choice of crops varies greatly throughout the region depending on soil, rainfall, and temperature conditions. African farmers are very skilled and understand their local

Price changes can greatly affect West African producers. Many farmers try to grow a range of different crops so that if the price of one crop falls they still have others to sell. Another reason for growing several crops is to guard against the risk of drought, disease or pests which can ruin one crop, but leave others untouched.

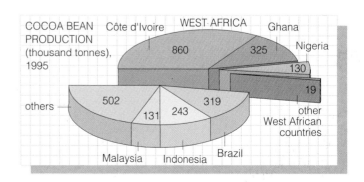

COCOA BEAN PRODUCTION (thousand tonnes), 1995

WEST AFRICA

Côte d'Ivoire 860

Ghana 325

Nigeria 130

other West African countries 19

others 502

Malaysia 131

Indonesia 243

Brazil 319

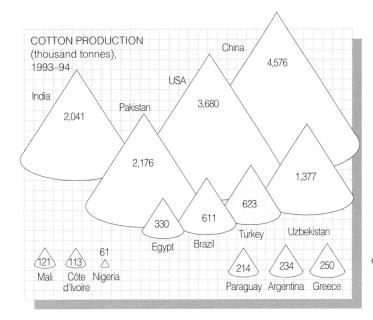

COTTON PRODUCTION
(thousand tonnes),
1993–94

China 4,576
USA 3,680
India 2,041
Pakistan 2,176
Uzbekistan 1,377
Turkey 623
Brazil 611
Egypt 330
Greece 250
Argentina 234
Paraguay 214
Mali 121
Côte d'Ivoire 113
Nigeria 61

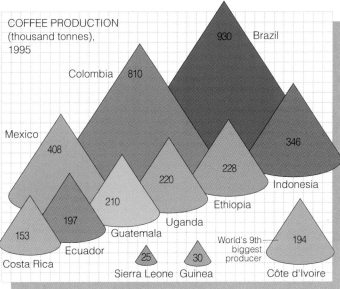

COFFEE PRODUCTION
(thousand tonnes),
1995

Brazil 930
Colombia 810
Mexico 408
Indonesia 346
Ethiopia 228
Uganda 220
Guatemala 210
Ecuador 197
Côte d'Ivoire 194 World's 9th biggest producer
Costa Rica 153
Guinea 30
Sierra Leone 25

environment at least as well as the best trained scientists. In many cases their knowledge is much greater. By growing crops with different water needs such as cassava, which requires very little water compared with maize, farmers can ensure that they will have some food even if the rains are poor.

Most farmers grow staple crops. These are crops that form the basis of the household diet, like wheat and potatoes in the UK and USA, or rice in much of Asia. West Africa's key staple crops are cassava, maize, millet,

rice, sorghum (guinea corn), and yams. In addition to these, farmers also grow vegetables such as sweet potatoes, chillies, tomatoes and beans, and various fruits including mangoes, bananas and paw paws. Farmers commonly plant a number of crops in the same field – a practice known as 'intercropping'. Apart from providing a more varied diet, the high density of crop cover also protects the soil from erosion during heavy storms. At first sight many fields look very disorganized, but experts

◀ *Fulani children patiently wait their turn to collect water from a rural water pump. It is usually the young girls who collect water for the home.*

FOOD AND
FARMING

◀ **Fish is a vital source of protein in the diets of many West African people. A catch of fish, landed in Ghana, is sorted out into different varieties before it is sold in the market.**

now agree that this method is, in fact, a good way of adapting to environmental conditions.

West Africans also eat meat from chickens, sheep, and goats and use milk

KEY FACTS

● Completed in 1976, the Tiga Dam, south of Kano in northern Nigeria, irrigates over 60,000 hectares of land on the Kano River Project, where crops such as wheat, rice and tomatoes are grown.

● Fanti fishermen from Ghana have migrated westward along the coast and settled in The Gambia. From a settlement called Ghana Town, they fish in the Atlantic Ocean for shark and ray which are then dried, salted and bagged before being sent home to Ghana.

● Ghana and Senegal are the main fishing countries in West Africa and, in 1992, they landed 427,000 tonnes and 327,000 tonnes respectively. This is important in the region but insignificant compared with the US catch of 5.6 million tonnes.

from cattle. Cattle are very important to African farmers and to many pastoral groups they are a symbol of wealth. The Fulani people, who range across the savanna and sahel regions of West Africa, are the main pastoral group. Today relatively few Fulani are entirely NOMADIC, and most have fixed settlements around which they grow crops. However, they still retain a strong attachment to their livestock and are renowned for their expertize. Milk, yoghurt and butter are sold by Fulani women and can fetch high prices in urban markets.

FISHING

The long Atlantic coastline fringing West Africa means that many people engage in fishing. The Fanti and Ewe people of southern Ghana are well known for their skills as fishermen. The vast wetlands of Mali's inland Niger delta and the Hadejia-Nguru region of north-eastern Nigeria also provide valuable fishing grounds, as do artificial lakes such as Lake Volta in Ghana and Lake Kainji in Nigeria. In the inland Niger Delta, the Bozo and Somono people are important fishing communities.

◄ *Women harvesting rice in The Gambia. It is estimated that women produce more than 70% of Africa's food.*

RURAL DEVELOPMENT

Many people have attempted to increase agricultural production and improve the living standards of rural people in West Africa. However, many development schemes have not succeeded because outsiders have not understood farming practices and the needs of local people. In The Gambia, for example, attempts to improve the production of swamp rice failed because it was assumed that rice farmers were men. In fact, rice in The Gambia is regarded by the Mandinka and Wolof people as a 'woman's crop' and it is the women who have a wealth of knowledge about its production and processing. The construction of dams, reservoirs and

▼ *With support from development agencies, in this case in Niger, women are very successful in producing staple foods such as millet and maize.*

irrigation schemes in semi-arid regions, such as northern Nigeria, has benefited some people but caused problems for others. Poor farmers have often been unable to buy land. Fulani pastoralists have lost valuable grazing areas and their migratory routes have been disrupted. These dams have changed the flow of the river, so that there is now no annual flood and fewer fish to be caught.

Some development projects, however, have been more successful, particularly where developers have worked closely with local people. In north-west Burkina Faso, the Mossi people have, for years, been laying lines of stones across their fields to prevent erosion. The main problem they faced was a shortage of stones, so a development agency has now provided a truck to transport stones from further afield to the Mossi villages. Women's groups in The Gambia have been given seeds and tools to grow vegetables during the long

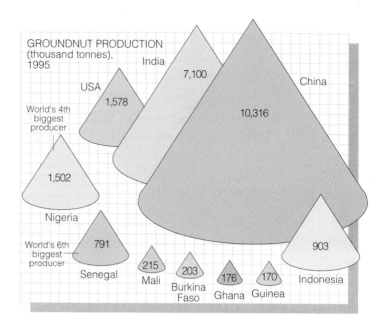

GROUNDNUT PRODUCTION (thousand tonnes), 1995

- India 7,100
- USA 1,578
- China 10,316
- Nigeria — World's 4th biggest producer 1,502
- Senegal — World's 6th biggest producer 791
- Mali 215
- Burkina Faso 203
- Ghana 176
- Guinea 170
- Indonesia 903

dry season. Wells have been sunk, and in some cases pumps driven by solar power have been installed to raise water on to the fields. The introduction of refrigerated trucks in the future could make it possible for vegetables to be transported long distances to the tourist hotels on the Atlantic coast, where demand is high.

▶ *Peppers for sale in a market at Onitsha, in southern Nigeria. Large food surpluses can be produced if the rains are plentiful and this is reflected in the many colourful markets throughout West Africa.*

TRADE AND INDUSTRY

Most West African countries continue to trade mainly with their former colonial power, for example 30% of Senegalese exports go to France and 37.8% of its imports come from France. Similarly, Ghana's main trading links are with the UK, with 13.8% of exports and 16% of imports. Despite ECOWAS attempts to promote trade within the region, relatively few goods are exchanged between different West African countries.

Large quantities of minerals (bauxite, iron ore, uranium, diamonds) and agricultural commodities (coffee, cocoa, cotton, groundnuts) are exported in a raw, unprocessed state. Processing is then mainly undertaken in European countries where, as a result, the value of the commodity is considerably increased.

SIERRA LEONE'S TRADING PARTNERS, 1995 (% of trade by value)

IMPORTS
others 38
Côte d'Ivoire 16.7
UK 16.7
USA 8.7
7.6
7.3
5
Netherlands
USA
Belgium/Luxembourg
India

EXPORTS
USA 19.6
Spain 12.8
UK 6
Germany 3.8
Portugal 3.8
Belgium/Luxembourg 19.6
34.4
others

KEY FACTS

● Tourism contributes over 12% of The Gambia's GNP and employs more than 35,000 people. The government is encouraging further expansion by giving free land to build hotels on the coast, and a new airport terminal was completed in 1997.

● Many of the poorer West African states rely heavily on official development assistance, or aid, from wealthier countries and international banks. In 1994, 70% of Guinea-Bissau's GNP was made up from aid receipts.

● Several countries in West Africa are heavily reliant on a single product. Niger relied on uranium for 65% of its export earnings in 1991, a 5% fall since 1978 due mainly to falling world prices.

◄ *Ports are the major focus for trade between West African countries and further afield. Dakar, in Senegal, is one of the region's major ports. When a new boat arrives, the port springs into life.*

◄ *A factory making plywood at Burutu, in southern Nigeria. Most of West Africa's agricultural products and minerals are exported in a raw state but countries can benefit considerably if they process raw materials locally.*

West African producers and producing countries usually receive only a small proportion of the value of the end-product.

Bottling plants for the soft drinks industry, where brands such as Coca-Cola are produced under local licences, are the most visible industries in many West African towns and cities. Food processing is also important. In Senegal, this accounts for almost half of industrial production and includes flour mills, a groundnut oil mill, a fish cannery, and a sugar refinery. Heavy industry is restricted to a few key centres, such as aluminium smelting in Ghana and Guinea, car assembly and petroleum refining in Nigeria.

Tourism is not as well developed in West Africa as it is in other parts of Africa. Although the region has tremendous potential, with its natural beauty, tropical sandy beaches, and fascinating cultural heritage, only relatively few areas have the necessary tourist hotels and INFRASTRUCTURE. An exception is The Gambia, which has invested heavily in package-tourism development, although it has only a 64-kilometre coastline. Ghana and the Casamance region of southern Senegal are also increasingly popular tourist destinations, but most other parts of West Africa are visited mainly by individual travellers.

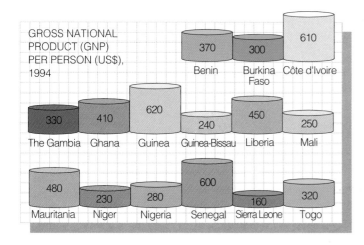

GROSS NATIONAL PRODUCT (GNP) PER PERSON (US$), 1994

			370	300	610
			Benin	Burkina Faso	Côte d'Ivoire
330	410	620	240	450	250
The Gambia	Ghana	Guinea	Guinea-Bissau	Liberia	Mali
480	230	280	600	160	320
Mauritania	Niger	Nigeria	Senegal	Sierra Leone	Togo

TRANSPORT

West Africa's transport system is poorly developed compared with those of Europe or North America. Although paved roads connect the main centres, many are in a poor condition and badly pot-holed, making travel in the rainy season particularly difficult. Few people own cars, so most use public buses or minibuses known variously as 'mammy wagons' in Nigeria and 'poda podas' in Sierra Leone. Road travel can be dangerous, with busy roads and poorly maintained and overcrowded vehicles, leading to fatal accidents.

Unlike east and southern Africa, railways are not well developed in West Africa. Railway routes were mainly constructed during the colonial period and tend to consist of single lines connecting coastal ports with important mines and cash-cropping areas. There are no railway links between French and English speaking countries. Only Nigeria has anything resembling a rail 'network', although, in the mid-1990s, only a few trains were operating because of lack of maintenance.

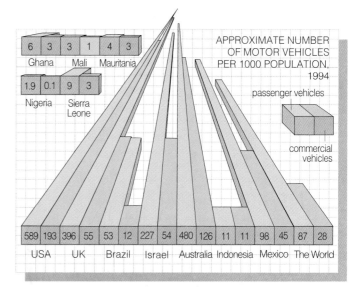

APPROXIMATE NUMBER
OF MOTOR VEHICLES
PER 1000 POPULATION,
1994

passenger vehicles

commercial vehicles

Ghana	Mali	Mauritania	Nigeria	Sierra Leone	USA	UK	Brazil	Israel	Australia	Indonesia	Mexico	The World
6 3	3 1	4 3	1.9 0.1	9 3	589 193	396 55	53 12	227 54	480 126	11 11	98 45	87 28

▲ **Unpaved roads can easily become impassable during the rainy season. Trucks often get bogged down for days at a time.**

◄ **A donkey cart is a prized possession for many poor rural families. People and goods can be carried to and from the fields and market.**

KEY FACTS

● Niger Republic, with an area of 1,267,000 square kilometres, has only 12,000 kilometres of roads and is more than 600 kilometres away from the nearest sea port at Cotonou in Benin.

● The proportion of paved roads in West Africa was just 19.5% in 1995 compared with around 60% in the USA and almost 100% in the UK.

● Ghana has two commercial deep-water ports at Tema and Takoradi. The government has received US$ 150 million from several overseas donors to modernize the ports for future expansion of trade.

There are also relatively few air passenger connections between former French and British colonies, but well developed links with European cities such as Paris and London. Air transport could be the best way of covering the long distances between the region's major cities, but the development of air travel has been limited by the high cost of running a national airline, and by the fact that many people cannot afford the fares.

Lagos, Abidjan, Dakar and Freetown are important West African seaports and are vital for importing and exporting bulky goods. Some new ports have been created, such as Tema in Ghana. Before the 1950s, Tema was a small fishing village, but now has a great artificial harbour constructed to serve the Akosombo Dam and Accra, the country's capital.

However, for most West Africans, who cannot afford to use expensive modern transport, the main means of travel are by bicycle, donkey cart or on foot. Village blacksmiths can easily make simple donkey carts out of recycled metal from disused vehicles.

▼ *For centuries goods have been transported along the River Niger in Mali in traditional boats known as 'pirogues'.*

THE ENVIRONMENT

West Africa has a number of bustling cities but also vast, sparsely settled, untouched areas. One major difference from eastern and southern Africa is that the West African region has very little large-mammal wildlife. Village elders, however, can remember when elephants, lions and other animals roamed the forest and savanna. Sadly, most have been killed by hunters or displaced by expanding human settlements. Today West Africa is famous for its bird life and, each year, a large number of ornithologists visit countries such as The Gambia to study resident and migrant birds.

West Africa's rapidly growing population has put great pressure on the environment. The main environmental problems are water shortages, pollution, deforestation, soil erosion and desertification. These problems

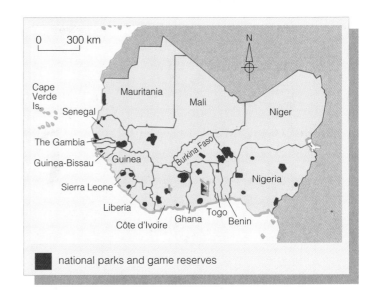

national parks and game reserves

are often closely related. For example, the clearance of tree cover for cultivation exposes the soil to a higher risk of erosion. Heavy rains may wash away nutrient rich top-soils, reduce fertility and lead to falling crop yields. Some people have suggested

◀ *Abuko Nature Reserve in The Gambia has been a long-standing example of how West Africa can preserve its remaining wildlife. The park is enclosed to protect it from encroaching settlement and farming.*

► *An African Darter is one of a wide variety of birds, native to this region, that can be seen in many of West Africa's national parks. Visitors also come to see the many birds that migrate to West Africa to escape the European winter.*

that these processes, over a prolonged period, may eventually lead to desertification. After one or two good rainy seasons, however, the growth of natural vegetation will sometimes restore fertility and reduce the threat of erosion.

In towns the main environmental problems are related to overcrowding and poor urban planning. Housing is often badly built and located haphazardly on any available land. Shortages of clean water and inadequate sanitation facilities are major problems, especially in overcrowded city slums. People are sometimes forced to drink water that may have been used for washing, cleaning clothes, and watering livestock. The region's major diseases, such as hepatitis, typhoid, dysentery and diarrhoea are transmitted through using dirty water. Malaria is transmitted by mosquitoes which breed near stagnant or slow-moving water. Infection rates are often very high in crowded slum areas. Many rural areas also lack safe water and sanitation facilities and people will use the nearest stream, river or lake for drinking water and washing.

Mineral exploitation can have a significant impact on the environment.

ACCESS TO SAFE WATER, 1990–96 (%)

Country	%
Benin	50
Burkina Faso	78
Côte d'Ivoire	75
The Gambia	48
Ghana	65
Guinea	55
Guinea-Bissau	59
Liberia	46
Mali	45
Mauritania	66
Niger	54
Nigeria	51
Senegal	52
Sierra Leone	34
Togo	63
China	67
Brazil	73
India	81
Japan	97
Vietnam	43

▶ **Refuse builds up around a market in Benin. The rapid growth of the cities means that services such as refuse disposal are often inadequate.**

◀ **On the outskirts of Freetown, Sierra Leone, local farmers have reclaimed land from the mangrove swamps. The local environment has been transformed and food is produced for both domestic consumption and for sale.**

◀ The Niger Delta, in Nigeria, has rich oil reserves but extraction can lead to severe environmental damage to the fragile wetlands.

local community action, such as the Naam movement founded, in 1967, in Yatenga Province, Burkina Faso. In this region with poor soils and frequent droughts, the Naam movement encourages local communities to work together in projects such as establishing fruit tree nurseries, planting trees to supply fuel and building dams to irrigate rice, vegetables, and fruit trees.

Open-cast tin mining on the Jos Plateau in Nigeria and diamond mining in Sierra Leone have led to widespread devastation of farmland. In the Niger Delta of Nigeria, major international concern, as well as complaints from local communities, have focused on pollution caused by drilling for oil. Farmers' crops have been ruined and intense gas flares burn constantly, close to villages. West African governments have started to recognize the importance of protecting their natural environments for future generations, and have set up several national parks to conserve both animals and their habitats from further destruction.

Local people are often more anxious to conserve the environment, since many of them directly depend on it for their livelihoods. There are many examples of

KEY FACTS

● In 15 years, Burkina Faso has lost nearly 60% of its trees through drought, over-grazing, bush fires and uncontrolled felling. The water table has fallen by around 20 metres in the last two decades.

● Between 1980 and 1989, Côte d'Ivoire cleared its forests at an average of 510,000 hectares per year or 5.2% of total reserves – one of the fastest rates in the world.

● Throughout West Africa, in 1996, only about 54% of the population had access to safe water and about 31% had adequate sanitation facilities.

● Small-scale illegal operations by local prospectors can cause serious environmental damage. In May 1992, about 100 people were killed when an illegally-dug diamond mine in Sierra Leone caved in.

● In 1997, Côte d'Ivoire decided to ban the ivory trade in order to limit the threats to its remaining elephant population of around 2,000. Côte d'Ivoire has the largest elephant population in West Africa after Nigeria.

THE FUTURE

◀ **Nigeria has spent millions of dollars in building the new capital city of Abuja in the sparsely settled 'middle belt' of the country. Government ministries and foreign embassies are gradually moving into the new city.**

West Africa is probably the poorest region in the world, with the worst life expectancy and infant mortality rates. The region and its people have a long way to go to catch up with their fellow Africans, let alone reach the standards of living enjoyed by the majority of people in North America or Western Europe. Some of the major development priorities for the future are ensuring clean water supplies, basic health care and primary education. Transport, electricity, and sanitation also need to be improved. As the population is growing so rapidly, particularly in the towns and cities, adequate food supplies and the provision of low-cost, high-density housing is a priority. It is important, too, that the rural areas are not neglected, since this is where most people live. If conditions are improved in the countryside, fewer people will want to migrate to the cities.

Little progress is likely to be made,

KEY FACTS

● With the exception of Guinea-Bissau, all of the West African countries are expected to double their population by the year 2020, if 1993 population growth rates continue.
● HIV is becoming a major threat to many of West Africa's people. In Ghana, by the year 2,000 it is estimated that there will be over 150,000 child orphans as a result of parents dying from AIDS.
● In 1997, scientists from America and Ghana signed a five-year agreement in Accra to research into a treatment for malaria, one of the region's major diseases.
● At a seminar on West Africa's natural resources, held in 1997, it was stated that West Africa's known reserves of oil and gas are so large that there is great scope for expansion if modern methods of extraction are used.

however, unless the region is politically and economically stable. Long-term planning has so often been interrupted by sudden changes of government. The West African people are, however, enterprising and resourceful and have a positive outlook on life. ECOWAS could point the way to future prosperity and a new spirit of co-operation between the West African states and their peoples. In late 1996, the Ghanaian, Kofi Annan, who worked for thirty years at the United Nations (UN) was elected Secretary-General of the UN by the General Assembly in New York. As a West African now occupies one of the most influential positions in the world, this may help to focus greater attention on the region in the future.

▲ *The University of Benin, in Nigeria. Education is valued highly in West Africa although many other levels, such as primary education, are still desperately short of resources.*

FURTHER INFORMATION

● NIGERIA HIGH COMMISSION,
9 Northumberland Avenue,
London WC2N 5BX
Provides general information on Nigeria.
● GAMBIA HIGH COMMISSION,
57 Kensington Court, London W8 5DG
Provides general information on The Gambia.
● GHANA HIGH COMMISSION,
13 Belgrave Square, London SW1X 8PR
Provides general information on Ghana.
● SENEGAL EMBASSY,
11 Phillimore Gardens, London W8 7QG
Provides general information on Senegal.
● WEST AFRICA PUBLISHING CO LTD,
43–45 Cold Harbour Lane, Camberwell
London SE5 9NR
Publishes a weekly current affairs magazine providing information on the region.

BOOKS ABOUT WEST AFRICA
● *Continents: Africa,* Colm Regan and Peter Cremin, Wayland 1996 (age 10+)
● *Africa: Eyewitness Guides,* Yvonne Ayo, Dorling Kindersley 1995 (age 10+)
● *Developing Geography: Ghana,* Birmingham Development Centre 1995 (age 11+)
● *World Focus: Senegal,* Ali Brownlie, Oxfam 1996 (age 12–14)

GLOSSARY

ARID
A word used to describe an extremely dry area that receives very little rainfall.

CASH CROPS
Crops which are grown mainly for sale in overseas markets, but which are also sold in local markets.

COLONIALISM
A system under which one country occupies and rules another country.

CULTIVATORS
People who grow crops for sale and to support themselves and their families.

DELTA
A flat, fan-shaped area of land where a river splits into many channels, usually as it empties into the sea.

DESERTIFICATION
The process whereby a piece of land becomes barren and infertile — like a desert. It can be caused by drought, deforestation, over-cultivation and soil erosion and is very difficult to reverse.

GROSS NATIONAL PRODUCT (GNP) PER CAPITA
The total value of all goods and services produced by a country in a year.

HYDRO-ELECTRICITY
Electricity produced by flowing water that drives a generator.

INDEPENDENCE
The transfer of power from a foreign colonial country to a government set up by local people who are then able to control their own affairs.

INFORMAL SECTOR
The section of the economy that involves people selling goods or offering services, sometimes in the streets or in markets, and which is often not officially recognized.

INFRASTRUCTURE
A network for transmitting and transporting such things as water, electricity, information or vehicles such as electricity pylons or a motorway.

LAGOON
A shallow area of water usually separated from the sea by a sand bar (sand bank).

LAND-LOCKED
A country, territory or area that has no coastline. Land-locked countries are highly dependent on their neighbours to reach coastal ports, which are important for trade and industry.

NOMADIC
A word describing a wandering lifestyle which is usually associated with livestock herders moving with their animals in search of pasture and water.

PASTORALISTS (PASTORAL GROUPS)
People who look after animals, sometimes moving long distances in search of water and grazing.

POLITICAL INSTABILITY
A situation where governments change rapidly, sometimes seizing political power by force in a 'coup d'état'.

RURAL-URBAN MIGRATION
The movement of people from rural areas to towns and cities, often in search of employment.

SAVANNA
A tropical vegetation consisting of grasses, shrubs and scattered trees. It is typically dry for most of the year but bursts into life when the first rains arrive.